ISADORA NEVES MARQUES

BIOGRAPHY OF A FICTION

BIOGRAPHY OF A FICTION

Fiction 1

What to write and
What not to write
The power of typing
Editing in and out
The people in your life
They have a say—

A scar

A scar on my left
blade, overgrown. Cut. I
wrote a fiction
for a piece of flesh.
Erotic disease and
the seasons.

After clouds, the sun.
We got good light—
shutter and gag reflex:
the aluminum enters
from the right. Cut.
The days seamlessly.

What else but to make myself
a character, and insert myself
where it hurts. Confessions
are not enough; rhythms, yes.
Finger tapping on skin, feels
like rubber.

It's a boy!

so early
the definition
of life

differentiation
in womb   the choice
is made
                     in advance
                     gender
                     is nothing
but a lump
                     in
                     rubber gloves
                     and ultrasound
                     gel

—it's a boy!

Prepubescence

Preadolescent mourning
The embryo

Before secondary sex characteristics
He lies in bed

Concerned with the afterlife
At midnight

Wasted Insemination

Came out
As young
Fulfilled

I'm gay, he said. Still

Sad over
A lack
Of children

Moon Erection

Reproduction
in the name of who?

If only men could draw
the moon nearer to them

tides would wash
their testes

round and round

Tides

The moon is a technology.

Ovarian implant

In the arm, close to the armpit, almost
there, in the belly, near the bellybutton,
in-between two abs, the experiment
was fictional, it worked, in his mind
something was growing.

hide behind an eye

falsify nothing
falsify everything
hide behind an eye
squeeze it
sometimes a baby pops out

The babies

The babies
The babies
The babies

The babies
The babies

The babies

Shove it in the belly

A conceptually driven series
                                        of lives

A row of hands holding
a cellphone
is the most intimate
                                        of things

Shove it in the slot, into the belly
bursts the white plywood wall

Speculation is freedom

What scares me
is not life as it is
but when fiction starts

your call
to turn reality
into otherworldly events

she said

speculation is freedom
but it is also a subterfuge
you hide in

The uses and abuses of a narrative

Is autofiction a masculine genre
regardless if written by men or women?

The uses and abuses of a narrative
centered on the I.

I swallow words that aren’t mine.

I put words in the mouths of others.

These words aren’t mine.

Interesting People

Don't be too
Interesting
Or you'll end
Up in
A story
I tell
Everyone I
Meet
When I first
Meet anyone

Privileges

I tried to refuse myself
the privileges
of an I
            but here am I.

If I write poems about me
            it's only because everything else I write
            is not about me.

Infancy

Remember his arm resting, limply
on the open window of the sports car?

Downstairs, it was early evening, in front of the high-rise
we used to live in, childlike like children—

I was a child. He was an adult.

Violence often happens within the family.

Repressed Memory

spoof—a bed that insists on being placed under the window
when what I recall is its place next to the door. Why does it insist
on being placed under the window? In that place
it faces the door, which opens in the shape of a silhouette,
but then is closed. I am facing the wall, napping under the window;
the bed shapeshifts into a bunkbed—the psychoanalytic reading:
a bunkbed means a couple, nearness, a shared space.
The odour of a giant beard. The frightening, soft
giant bear—its eyes pierce me, again and again
the bed slips—the bear pierces me

A storm

the day a storm
flooded the house
abuse washed away

Crisis on Infinite Earths

A life like a child
Is tapping for sense
Across Infinite Earths

On this earth
Death is the size of a universe
Collapsed on a bed, possibly

A Surgery

Back to school with a hidden scar—
the conscious tactility of confusion
on the verge of sexuality.

I used it rarely, pulling hard as allowed
a failed genital—the undefined exacerbation
of an organ.

Cut the edges of familiarity—
the routines of satisfaction
made uncanny.

Calf

Felt the skin tremble.
Peel the fur from the calf
        that sees itself still
        as a child unmoving
        in time.

        Felt is a warm feeling.

Features predestine little

I was fine, fragile, feminine
a word chosen, as a child—

What was wrong with feminine anyway?

Oh, was it a dangling feeling in-between?

I masturbated it curiously, and made of myself a man.

The pretense of puberty

Fearful of female laughter, I forced my hips
into a just discovered masculinity. Meanwhile
behind the sports pavilion a row of boys
comparing degrees of stiffness—I was
neither here nor there, unaware
of the impossibility of in-betweeneness. Drips
of excitement in the showers, confessions
homoerotically repressed. And the girls
were all so farcical; how could I not love them?

Best Friend

Best friend
at sixteen Redraw your
biography Backward
memories A boy
came for me

Magik

I did not desire magic
I wanted to be magic

Stepping discs
Across a failed infancy

Take me back seven years
in as many seconds
Magic turned old

Watching a mansion from afar in the pure,
having just fallen snow

Behind the window shades, puberty

at night death is a neighbor

at night death is a neighbor
eyes fixed on outer space

I was the child who saw nothing
and questioned what Nothing was

in the movie *The Neverending Story*
Nothing consumes all—

the Earth reduced to an island
floating in metaphysical space

Childhood conjecture

All the things I never did
I didn't do because I was sick
for a long time; but before that
I wasn't.

Now remembering those early years
when falling I fractured my nasal bridge
confirms me a childhood conjecture—

then later came the spells
and the endocrinology departments;
a light touch on the neck, two fingers on each side,
the thought became the focus of my attention:

it both comforted and paralyzed me.
I incorporated it in my bodily movements;
then people noticed, and called back, chased me—

I've come to love my body

I've come to love my body, in its density, compactness,
                                        fibrous muscularity
                                        of chest and hamstrings

while missing, longingly, the body I imagined
                                        as a child, the female
                                        I carry in memory

Queer Changes

Queer
Changes
In time
Change
Chances
For
Queer
Changes

Fiction II

fiction

is a game of perspectives

a field called reality

at intervals

This poem should self-reflect #1

This poem should self-reflect

And
Spin the particles of self

Inside my own private
Hadron collider

Seven and a half times around the globe
At the speed of 35 years/time

Hard to fathom
The multiplication of universes
We opt out of

This poem should self-reflect #2

This poem should self-reflect

The hypothesis of birthing
Change

In multiplication of
Tense strings

The lived bonds and imagined
Conflicts

Bellies burst
In the attempt
Of sensing

This poem should self-reflect #3

This poem should self-reflect

And
Stress the exercise of redundancy

Build ever larger colliders
62 miles wide, protons traveling underwater

BOOM
And all that falls is crap

Wet particles
Wear my innards
Down to parties

Kitty Pryde

in every possible direction
                    there are meanings
                    and desires
                    defensively
                    misinterpreted
                    into reasoning,
                    such as
                    caring for the wrong
                    ones, ones
                    and zeros are not
                    enough;
                    feelings are fluid,
immaterial   Kitty Pryde
                    crossing firm walls
                    in the 80s
                    turning pages
                    I wished I could be a spirit
                    like her
                    colored in pencil
                    in the sewers
                    mutants were
                    being
                    hunted down

A childhood called AIDS

1.

my first image of sexuality was AIDS
so early, the legacy of disease

three twelve-year-olds masturbating on a suburban couch
while I retreated—sperm was death

2.

sex on tv, "time for bed," dad said;
peeping through a half-shut door at night

tv taught me the imperative of choice:
better a woman than a man

3.

AIDS wasn't simply sexed bodies, or my sex,
the realization that I had one at all
it was also the intercourse between skin and environment

fearful of needles in the beach sand, fearful of playgrounds
fearful of fun and of other children's bodies

4.

puberty offered me neither hair nor muscles, like other boys'
but I was learning a new vocabulary, like white blood cells

even when by oneself, imagination
found its way to death

5.

the rectum is a grave
I explored anality with cocktails of spit and fear

fearful of holes, fearful of penises
fearful of fluids and of the rawness of binaries

6.

AIDS was the trauma and the paranoia of children
who wished only to love

without confusing virginity
with death

Memory

I connect
every little detail
to disease
and then back
to memory
every day, like the days
I recall
feeling sickly, and the days
before I
felt sick, before
I was an I
becomes you
and never let's go

Ghost

I lived with a ghost throughout my twenties.
It was a very heavy ghost; it used to hang from my neck.

Now in my thirties, I still live with that ghost, but it is not as heavy.

I remember its touch on my neck,
that rubbery feeling; I remember the touch more than the thing.

So I call it a ghost—what were you thinking?

I have no issue with ghosts, as long as ghosts have no issues with me.

Thyroid

My thyroid drapes south off my feet, and then roots me.
The earth never lets us go, and is often moist.

Chronically we move on

Chronically we move on.
There is no going back
To a time I endured
Alone, even when
In company, even when
In love.

Writing is the only way
To connect—not bring back, I
Don't write to bring back anyone—
A wide-eyed child with
The adult, one day, I found
That child was gone. And I was old.

I know who you are

you become someone
you do not wish for so fast
you start meeting people and
they mean nothing, names and
faces, someone tells you,
I know who you are.
you do not trust them.

Restaurant at the End of the Universe

Dining by yourself at the end of the universe—
the soup is heavy and you are many

A foreword

As for this here, before you
better not say much. Only that I am in there
them, these poems:

a foreword that in turn
turns into
regurgitation.

timeless

if there were
no futures
nor pasts
there
would be
no neuroses

The Early Death of Sigmund Freud

by the by, travel back in time

to kill Freud

it would've saved us some trouble

A living being

A living being
Inside one's head, it's not easy

When the head is a world
And the world is imagination

Perishability is not an issue
But old age would be fair.

Without present there is
Neither past nor future—

Time flows naturally;
There is sameness between parent and child.

child growth

will the child grow
to be something else than genes?

a child always grows
in too small a house

flimsy walls

My mom almost fell

Once dad opened the car door
while driving on the highway
my mom almost fell
on the asphalt, it was night
but during daytime
I dreamt
in the backseat
the emotions
I once felt
return, surreptitiously
like the traits and facial expressions
the receding hairlines and
disillusioned stares
of dad. I surprise myself
at this persistence:
sure, genes have their ways
but what about a child
who wishes to become a writer
and then becomes a writer?
I feel haunted—
the many roads I've taken
have only led me back to where I started;
the same ancestral shame, the same
awe at the world
I know, that much I can acknowledge,
the path has been sincere.

Maturity

The tongue rolls with maturity—what is adulthood but a private infancy?

Fiction III

Do I persist?
    When the border is your life
    and mine is but a testimonial.

    I persist
    across the border
    to a land where I'm secondary.

    Tell me
Am I saying too much?

    I did not ask for consent
    to write you into my life.
    If you, now, place a demand on me
Should I go back in time?

I expect to be a center

Even in dreams, a third person.
I don't ask for the details of a face,
as I expect to be a center. An expression
of interest, blurry yet guaranteed—happenstance
delivered in three months or six years:
it makes no difference. I expect to be a center.

Substitutes

She fingers him from behind.

He imagines she isn't her.

She pretends and plays the part.

He moans sadly, because she knows.

Afterwards, she cries.

The uses of a body

How unconscious was I
when during all those years
you not once used me
like an object.
How tame.
How peaceful.
How mechanical
the passions of my body.

Separate beds

I remember a house, many years ago,
with separate single beds and a couple sleeping
with a table in-between. Resting sideways
he watches her on the opposite bed
sleeping with someone else.

Child with no genders

if we had had a child
we would've had a child
with no genders

even when you didn't
want a child, you still respected
my imagination

sometimes, even now, I
stay behind, and we fuck
as promised the bond is strong

unprotected, when
she comes and stays
for yet another night

I hollow and realize
the mourning
is mine

A Rogue and a Gambit

We, as in an individual
locked into plural

That was the reality I faced and a fear

A rogue and a gambit lose their edge
when forced into coupledom

After a while a couple becomes individual:
two atoms constrained by telepathy

As time passed, the fear turned into choice

So I placed my cards on the table, charged
with immensity, and went on to absorb other lives

Slow Learner

I am
    a slow learner
        of odd chances

translation

always translating

stories heard
and stories told
only to hear
those stories
were mine
to begin with

I tend to forget—no mind

hurt
some
times
occurs

Alien Abduction

For Alice dos Reis

Alien abduction stories
were pregnancy stories
in a time of IVF

and assisted reproduction
little green men
at work inside women's bodies.

Scully bled from her nose
after she got abducted by aliens.
I was terrified, as a child
the blood dripping down
her lips
was—her flow?

An abortion?

I had bad dreams.

Gay Dads

For a while I searched for a gay man
with a child, so I could go on with my life
knowing I'd gotten the full package

I didn't find a man
so I wrote a story
about a pregnant man

Later I realized that man didn't have to be gay
and I didn't have to be a man

The baby is waiting

Wrote a conversation about an unborn
baby, not knowing whom the baby belonged to.

Him?

The baby is waiting
in the wrong womb.

Nine Months

An exercise in cuts
may just bring forth many
                                        children

what a joy a nine-month
                                        interruption

How many eggs are in
these lives   I've written
             myself into a corner

now all I've got is imagination

Therapist

She says,

Having a child would free you
from yourself.

My therapist says,

Your problem is your mind
is always active.

I answer,

The thing is I can't have a child
by myself.

My therapist tell me,

That's all in your mind.

Reproduction is also this

The revelation of sameness and the repetition of
difference—the word
my therapist claims
I repeat, in order to define myself.

Now, physically I know
I am uncapable of gestation—
but reproduction is also this:
to speak is to exist.

Mistranslation

The Portuguese language is full of hidden meanings.
Inside each word a world.

In the Portuguese language *género* means gender.
It also means genre.
The same word is full of double meanings.

Which genre to talk about gender?
Which gender to talk about genre?

If the word is imprecise, so will the world.
And that can only be a good thing when talking
about the promiscuity between genre and gender.

parody

a certain parody occurs

when the genre is wrong

and the translation impossible

Bodies

I'm incapable of
                    measure
only   of
the discomfort
and
the pendulum
                    trapped in
          the sway

of being in the body I am
          and the body to become

The Division

My body is rubbery, my mind hard.
I don't believe in the existence of either—
that is, in their separation. Still, I suffer in the division.

pills

despite decades of equilibrium
nonetheless discomfort

when fog clouds
the mind
weakens, I doubt

prescription pills
swallowed

Smile

What's the humor of depression?

a dry
vague
uninterested
humor
but a humor no less

Brain—Soul

Brain Soul

Two words.
So short and simple.

Not that much of a difference in meaning either.

Still,

they remain words
worlds
apart.

Turn the monster against itself

Turn the monster
within
Give it a name

How often the pretense
of daily business
It goes on forever

The routines
on which we operate
an exercise of depersonalization

A moment
erupts from the chest
The metaphors we use

The mark of difference
in the silence
of a stare

The life I couldn't live
Sobbing in a public cubicle
while traveling at the speed of light

Health is an imaginary
limit
First steps toward peace

Turn the monster
against itself
And make a mantra of acceptance

The world is not what it seems

The world is not what it seems. It is wider
than the mind. And the politics that shape the mind.

Gonads

go do an
hormonal exam

No matter
how late. What
was I when young
percentages dictate
desire
but remain nothing but
percentages

go na ds
are strong

The Wrong Sex

Find your place. You're a fish in a pond.
Be a fish.

Tailbone

A woman has no organs.

A man has no organs.

Neither women nor men have any organs.

In the beginning there was neither

gap nor lack

no overcompensation

like the tailbone we lost

in womb

leave the difference behind.

two-star system

gender duality
online—nature
docs streaming—
even in alien worlds
the division rules—

Darwin's cameo—
despite outer space
predatory violence
pervades imagination—
a narrow worldview—

dreaming of sexuality
beyond competition—
I cherish a two-star system—
take both the red
and the white dwarf home

Family Tree

I fought for a name at twenty
and swapped families, because
I had many names

Like a slow-tempered sword
axing
The family tree
That tree I knew existed
had asked to see
but never bothered to visit

Years hence—gosh, I'm almost 40
Perhaps it was never about the tree

Let's write
"Pedro"
and hear
how
dead
it sounds

Traveling through the gates #1

For Rachel Pollack
—that warm afternoon in Rhinebeck,
before she passed yet another portal

Like a fantasy character
Blocking the gates to the castle

With a heart of someone
Who has seen many

Men and women
Travel through the Beatrix Gates

Signed copy, elder
Approved

Traveling through the gates #2

He said,
I am not the gatekeeper

His voice solemnly controlled
The story I told

What changes are you looking for?
And I felt like being at the shopping mall

Unsure of what to buy, confused
Between pleasure and the strictly necessary for survival

Traveling through the gates #3

I came to the gates in fear
But on the other side I found only mirrors

Every little detail matters for a child
The differentiation of gendered roles as a teenager

I dreaded my best friend's precocious beard
I found comfort in the odor of passion

Did you feel different?
Yes, but then I became an artist

Clues

shoot it sideways, watch
their eyes chase
for clues

Time Travel

I time travel, after lunch
And openly reflect
The sexuality I am in

The sweet and sour
Aspect of post-orgasmic
Waste, on you

The revelations
Of a brief death

Moon and Nudity

Tucking myself, cross-gendered
stars, under the moon, freshly bathed,
the night is a buzz, insects wake, sun disappears,
satellites roam the sky, punctuated, space
revelations hit me. I become.

Fiction IV

I have taught myself to walk
round and round
fiction

After all, am I not meant to exercise?

As I approach
fiction, fiction
escapes further

NPC

I am a NPC in a lively landscape;
I observe, I gesticulate, I comment
when asked to comment.   All else is repose.

On people who've lived many lives and people who remain the same

I read an essay
on people who've lived
many lives and people
who remain the same

since childhood
for some is a perfect
set of events
for others it is barely an image

Clearly, to fake
a memory
is an act of growing
old

choice
is hardly given
when one remembers
little

To my mind I've changed
but I respect
the continuity
when it's pointed out to me

Home

The false idea that home is where one is born.

Truthfully, friends try to convince you to stay

And give a random place an original meaning.

Success

Where I was born, success, I was born
        but not much else

I remain a passing thought
        hardly reflected upon

                and of all that was gained
why do dreams weigh heavier
than these summer rains of late?

Arrogance

I'm not as smart as people think.

The Hill

Landing—the airplane
combs the air; agitated
suburban rooftops.

Childhood spent
watching airplanes disappear
behind a hill.

What is destiny?
Chasing fireflies
across borders.

Adulthood spent
observing fantasies harden
on the hill.

Departing—the spaceship
rumbles; humble
over high-rises.

What is illusion?
Chasing fireflies
across borders.

You will accept all

You will accept all that
has transcribed and all that will be

such as the sunrise—
even on foggy days
well, it is still a sunrise

and the moon—
even when clouded
well, it too is still a rock in the sky

Painting

I keep my memories safe.
They are painterly
Slices of color, brushed in humble tones.
Exodus is an inner travel.

Banality

To live is a banality.

In writing I strive to do justice to what was beautiful

Now I return to memory, always this
autobiographical poetry, who does it serve?

The cities we accumulate
are made of still images
lost on phones and loves long-departed   left
unfinished

I remember a good pose, and the amusement
of an audience
at the time sincere

Now we barely speak

With the years I confuse the minutia
with the big picture

In writing I strive to do justice to what was beautiful

Fiction v,
or
Fiction always wins

In a world where everything is a matter of fiction—truth
tends to arise always too late. And still
truth does not last—fiction always wins

Finally, we are the same

My breasts a symbol of life and death, embodied in vanity. The vulnerability of womanhood attached to sanctuary. The expected fear of abandonment, the deformations of skin. A pleasure prolonged through comparison. The same death, experienced henceforth, in distinct bodies at birth.

Variations on a body by comparison

The description of a body that is no longer mine,
but which is still capable of a past pleasure; she avoids it.
The issue is not the pleasure, then, but its image.

The desire to be humiliated by what you once were

The desire to be humiliated by what you once were—
acceptable only for as long as difference is maintained.
In other words, not as sameness. The men
and the women I've let in, the women especially
determined by a predilection admired by low pitch—
symbolisms of submission sought in spoken word.

The booming voice of men

How booming the voice of men;
raspy and strong
masculinity easily inversed
were it not for a culture of reprisal
at the flakiest sign of sensibility. Meanwhile
I observe a manly occupation of a space
I once called mine—I lie: it really wasn't
or vocal depth would not disturb me as much.

Men reaching maturity at 40

Spam of space—
An immensity filled with thrust
Pushing and pulling
Curiosity:
How did I arrive?
Newborn and strenuous
Stubborn
At young age.
A sensibility withheld by intelligence,
I did not know there was such a thing as too much of it.
Arrogance put to the page,
I wrote letters to myself
But failed lamentably at diaries—
Vanity, pure and simple and quite banal
Where is all of it now?
Accumulate wealth
Buy a house
Marry
Raise a child
None of these arrived or will they.
The comparisons of middle age,
Friendships that nonetheless break you—
And the years, of course, move on.
There is such a thing as relativity,
The question is how to live it.
I should know
Because I read stories of the multiverse
And of lives not lived.

Do I overthink?
Sure, I overthink.
The particularities of a poem are problems
Hardly solved early on,
Like men reaching maturity at 40.
Where does that leave me?

Astral Plane

We make an appointment to meet in the astral plane.
So I wake up early and meditate.

I pay no mind to my style of meditation,
because there is no mind to pay attention to.

A paradox arises from the silence:
how could we ever meet if there is no one to meet?

While love is absorbing a partner

While love is absorbing a partner
another love matures.

Past Lives

I tell you about W. B. Yeats, who also believed
he'd met his lover in a past life.

You say you've had a busy spiritual summer
and are now more in the mood for drinks.

Love does not suffice for the erotic

When love becomes taboo, all we do is talk about sex.
Sex is an image without remorse, easy
as withdrawal into necessity; successful yet insufficient
for the banality of a brittle commitment, what
we might call romantic love. Ever so gentle my education:
to be a good person, to want to be a good person
and yet remain the object of a forgotten movement.
This comfort of a liberal choice, open to the minutia
of physical traits and private tastes, a sincerity
so generous to the point of feeling contractual:
neither charisma nor deliverance.
Love does not suffice for the erotic.
And infant traumas are easy excuses—
avoidant, attached, anxious—
therapy grasped on a smartphone
mindlessly refreshed, the counseling—
recovery, repair, reunion—representation
of eroticism nullified by emotional intensity;
the blockage of streamed pornography
all leading up to you.

Obsession

A world of distance in a bowl of soup.
The borders we built. The judgements.
The characters we played. Over the phone
I declare my faith in fiction, and in private
my imagination takes the shape of a novel, repeated,
boringly, in variations all leading up to the same.

Why bother with fiction?

We strive for equality, but fiction has a cruel tendency to surprise even the fairest of plots.

Marriages fail.
Children bail on you.
Love ends in betrayal.
Families fall apart.

The Sex of Angels

Science is like arguing about the sex of angels.
Argumentation is necessary, yes, but let angels be angels.

A week in a couple's life

On Monday we marry,
On Tuesday we divorce.
On Wednesday we have babies—and babies go on forever.
On Thursday conflict is just a thing that happens.
Friday we break up. Saturday the wind stops
and there is such stillness we run back to each other's arms.
On Sunday God rested and we attend a mass neither of us believes in.

Moving out

The next-door apartment is vacant.
The landlord came to empty it the other day
and left the door open. Now the door stands ajar, sometimes
I glimpse inside it. It is used like a squandered marriage.
Maybe it's a sign for me to move in. One day, I left someone
inside my apartment, locked the door and threw away the keys.
I am given the choice to restart it all over again.

worry

you say I worry too much
about an I; in other words, you say
worry fills my pages with other lives—

the reality of an emptiness at the center of a poem that is full

Fiction VI, *or* *When change comes, embrace it*

What comes first?
Fiction or life?
When change comes
Embrace fiction.
While both are built
On memory, life
Can’t travel back in time.

I tell you this story

I am but a mental image of friends and family in mourning,
and after that the image of a second generation
who'll recall an extraordinary thing or two, followed by a third
for whom I'll be, at best, a scholarly rarity, a line of text
in an old forgotten book. In four generations
my accomplishments will be all but forgotten.
I tell you this story. And console myself
with a maturity always on the verge of arriving.

Aging

Aging—no concern.
What is skin if not a feeding ground;
traditional carps come out to eat

lovers' feet,
lovers' nails,
lovers' leftovers.

And where there are fish
there are turtles, warming
their shells in the sun.

Turtles walk slowly
but slowly, slowly
their tastes change.

I'd like to narrate myself through the lens of love

I'd like to narrate myself through the lens of love.
And to be honest. What else
left to offer but the bravery of the little things
that mourn us; a transparency
neither aggrieved nor grateful.
Uncertainties kept in a diary.

The Four Virtues

What value is there in a private confession?
    Worlds imagined but left unshared.
    I am learning techniques to abate subjectivity;
    such as, turning dialogues into a monologue,
    my voice solidified in the solitude of one's own gaze.
What is the exercise of subjectivation?
    Personifying someone other than ourselves on the page
    and in the empathy project our own desires
    on the sly. Now I follow the rules of citation.
In shutting ourselves out from others, do we lose?
    What do we lose?
    It is impossible to narrate the fullness of an experience
    just like the self we think ourselves to be is just a self among many,
    our treasured singularity imperfect outside of a collective.
Is autofiction in vogue because we are afraid of hurting each other?
    Or is it because we have grown comfortable with the abuse?
    Violently irresponsible in our individualization
    we privatize ourselves and call atomization respect.
But what of the resentment found in a confession?
    In therapy I learn not to speak for another;
    always say I feel, and so and so
    I have become a master of psychology, and so and so
Why the suffering?
    Free to narrate every tiny detail
    except if the orgasm was fake or real
    I humble myself, and study the four classical virtues.

I rest my case in the personal

I rest my case
in the personal;

there is much
to learn
in being quiet:

humility, for example,
is a teacher. I prefer
a seat at the back
where the exit is nearest.

How I stopped avoiding the news

After a perennial phase of avoiding the news, I find myself
cured of traditional anxieties. Not that the denial of reality
is a better reality than a muted one, but at least now I am better
informed. I know what occurs in faraway countries;
wars waged and commercial breakthroughs; the science
of relationships and advice on friendship. It's all the same.
The issue was never the news, of course—as with everything
it was always the analogies.

Lives lived

For some, life is a straight line;
for others it's a long, deep curve.
Or maybe I'm wrong
and straight lines tend to bend
at dramatic points
or when pushed to the limit;
just as curves are, to a certain extent,
if so wished, parallel, plain, and predictable.
I know both instances. I see myself in both.
And I have seen lines that do not cease to amaze me.

The Poverty of Poetry

The poverty of poetry is
to be alone in one's own thoughts
and not exist as a dialogue—
I thread along
the threshold between us.

I concede to consent—
an understandable demand—
and learn not to pull you in;
paraphrase
each spoken word.

These poems have become so self-obsessed
I keep failing them any exteriority—
references
obliquely leading back to me.
What worth is erudition?

Easier to say we live inside a simulation

How common to place ourselves inside a fiction.
A novel twenty years in the making, only to be left
unfinished, because incongruous now. And while
I shelved my story, I hold on to mental images
of those long, hopeful, negligible years.

I remember earlier, an arousal
I think of consciousness. But then waiting half a lifetime
to make sense of the narrative, in all likelihood out of touch
with reality—an autobiography
only now doubtful of facts.

More than the actuality of a body aging
I am now at peace with platitudes, such as
we are as many as those we interact with.
Easier to say we live inside a simulation; or believing that
an inquiring mind inside a head is thought—

Purely all that exists. Either this
or my mirror is askance, only partially reflecting
a landscape beyond the contours of logic, half-grasping
some old, familiar solid. Something like that.
Something incredible.

The Efficiency of Fiction

What's in a name
that changes constantly?
At each name change
identity falters, flaky
and insufficient. A hollowed
reputation. Concepts
thin and transparent as
glass, easily tilted and shattered.
You just have to keep moving.
The efficiency of a fiction is found
in the control of a narrative.

Isadora Neves Marques
Biography of a Fiction

Published by
After 8 Books, Paris

With the support of
FRAC Île-de-France
Galleria Umberto Di Marino, Napoli

Edited by
Benjamin Thorel

Design
Marco Caroti

Distribution
France & Belgium:
Interart, Paris, www.interart.fr
United Kingdom:
Art Data, London, www.artdata.co.uk
Rest of Europe:
contact us at orders@after8books.com
The Americas, Asia, Australia:
DAP | Distributed Art Publishers, New York, www.artbook.com

ISBN: 978-2-492650-18-5
Dépôt légal: décembre 2025
Printed in Estonia

THANK YOU *to all the real lovers, friends, and family in my life—you seem so unreal most of the time. Thank you for the loving learning curve Alice dos Reis. Thank you André Romão and Gonçalo Gama Pinto for always having your door open for me. Thank you for the trust João Moura and Luís Silva. Thank you for conversations across three continents Filipa Ramos, Mirene Arsanios, and Priyanka Sen. Thank you João Concha for publishing my poetry back "home." Thank you for the support Galleria Umberto di Marino and the di Marino family. Thank you to my parents—I am too absent.*

ISADORA NEVES MARQUES *is a poet, film director, and artist. They are the author of the poetry collections* A Campa de Marx *(Não Edições, 2025) and* Sex as Care and Other Viral Poems *(Pântano Books, 2020). They published short story collections such as* Morrer na América *(Kunsthalle Lissabon & Abysmo, 2017), and edited several projects on art and theory with Archive Books, Sternberg Press, and e-flux journal. Their films and artworks have been exhibited globally, from Cannes Critics' Week and the International Film Festival Rotterdam to Castello di Rivoli Museo d'Arte Contemporanea, Pérez Art Museum Miami, Centro de Arte Dos de Mayo, and Kyoto City University of the Arts Art Gallery, among many others. With artist Alice dos Reis, they co-founded the poetry press Pântano Books in 2020.*

BIOGRAPHY OF A FICTION *collects poems written between 2020 to 2025. These poems were written in a diaristic way, mostly in short form, while working on larger pieces, some of which also collected here or elsewhere. What started, seemingly, as notes on reproductive desire, gender, and sexuality soon matured into a meditation on the role of fiction in the exercise of writing (and idealizing) a biography, including the thorny aspect of artistic license and the uses of one's own life and of others. I hope you find some value in it.*

— ISADORA NEVES MARQUES